TELLING IT AT A SLANT

JOE NEAL

Pen Press

First published in Great Britain by Pen Press

All paper used in the printing of this book has been made from
wood grown in managed, sustainable forests.

ISBN13: 978-1-78003-664-9

Printed and bound in the UK
Pen Press is an imprint of
Indepenpress Publishing Limited
25 Eastern Place
Brighton
BN2 1GJ

A catalogue record of this book is available from
the British Library

Cover design Jacqueline Abromeit
Author on Cnicht, North Wales
Black and white photo by Justin Neal

ABOUT THE AUTHOR

Joe Neal was born half-way up a mountain in North Wales. He began his acting career in repertory theatre before attending Nottingham University. To supplement his income, he also trained as a journalist, working for the Western Mail, Times, Guardian, Daily Telegraph and Daily Express.

Described by director Jonathan Miller as "a sparky, idiosyncratic character actor," he has performed on stage, radio and television in Britain and Ireland. Between acting work Neal writes extensively on the countryside and natural history as well as devoting time to poetry and short stories which he believes should be read aloud – "even to oneself."

A glutton for punishing experiences, he stood twice as an independent for Parliament in Britain and once in the EU elections for Ireland's eastern constituency of 11 counties.

His published work has appeared in the Times, Daily Telegraph, Countryman, Ireland's Own, Waterlog, New Writer, New Society (now defunct), Scaldy Detail and numerous poetry magazines. Performed writing includes *Revenge*, *The Reluctant Trombonist*, *Send in the Clown* and *Kites and Catullus*.

Neal is presently living in Ireland. He is divorced and has one son – and now a grandson and daughter-in-law. *Telling It at a Slant* is his first book of poems – also available as a recording.

To the memory of my brother Richard

TALES FROM THE HEART AND OTHER PLACES

NOT SO BLIND

He arrived by car,
the blind piano tuner,
and tapped his way
to our front door,
while his stone-deaf wife
waited in the driving seat.
Sight and sound, they made
a grand duet –
but he didn't need
her eyes to render
discord into concord
on my father's Bechstein.

Peeping through the half-closed
door, I saw him play a note
and disappear behind
the shiny propped-up lid,
plucking at a wire
until the jagged sound grew round,
fading then to a soft caress;
in sight again, he'd feel
his way back to the stool,
stabbing at a key
or playing a chord
until he found another
noise his ear
could not tolerate.

1

He took so long –
tweaking, twanging,
thumping, banging –
and the repeated notes
up and down the scale
were annoying to the ear;
then, suddenly, came
harmonies so sweet
that I closed my eyes,
mesmerised,
as he conjured colour
out of black and white;

I was perfectly in pitch
with my insighted, sightless
friend – and knew he saw
another standing there:
"That's the sound
of music, boy," he said
towards the door,
"now fetch your dad to me."

SLEEPER

Across the carriage from me
she lay
asleep
her peculiar beauty
came from the hint
of a puckered mouth
testament to the soft approach
of middle age

In my thoughts I leaned across
and kissed those lips
and felt her stir her hips
yes
that's what I missed
at nights
not just the passion
it's that tenderness
that soft and yielding comfort
that awakens another hunger
just as strong

Then I caught her glance
lips slightly parted
she looked at me

"your money and your life"
she seemed to say
(challenging)
for there was much on offer

And then I laid it on the line
soon my luck will change
si vis suppeditat
(begging now)
there's just a chance

It was then that she turned
to regard me
at a distance
safely round the world's circumference

My dreams had fled
hers
not even started

YOU'RE NEVER ALONE WITH A SPIDER

I call her Ida,
my six-legged spider;
you see, I checked her out
in my arachnid book
and know she's of the fairer sex;
but how she lost two
shapely legs she cannot tell.

With four one side and two
the other, she cuts a dashing
curve across the floor and ends
up near her starting point,
where she waits awhile
to regain strength for yet
another paralympic scurry.

Thinking it's the bathroom
that she wants – and a sip
of water from the tub –
I place a saucer within
six paces of her
reluctant-insect form, and wait.

Two hours later she's still
standing there, and the saucer's dry.

Did she take a lick while
I wasn't looking?
Or did the water
just evaporate?
Like with the missing
legs, I'll never know for sure,
but this is what I think
about her accident:

One giant step it took
to pin my spider to the floor,
but she gamely struggled
free, losing two limbs
above the hairy knee.
Little wonder, then,
that she's reluctant
to court more danger
from this human stranger.

Each day I find her
in the room, I count
my blessings – and hers too,
and yearn to see her grow
another pair;
but she's no regenerating
worm and, besides,
I wouldn't know her then.

So I speak to her
and hope that little
by little my Ida

will learn a spider
trust of me;
my voice, her silence,
what a perfect combination!

KILN RAIDERS

When we were picking
stones to help prepare
the hockey pitch,
we boys and girls found
pottery and green-aged
coins with Caesar's head
staring from a distant
past of Roman occupation.

Of course, we pocketed
our plundered trove
before museum people
came to dig the spot,
uncovering a kiln
where Marcus, Gaius
or Octavius had turned
and thumbed a wheel
of clay and baked a pot.

I still have my shard
of curving rim
and wonder if I own
the last remaining
jigsaw piece
of amphora to make
Exhibit One complete.

DENIAL

I wanted to remember
her alive – not dead,
but the coroner insisted:
"You must identify her," he said.
But it wasn't her
I saw so still
behind the curtain;
not my Mum,
my Daddy's darling Rosie
who hugged me each night
I went to bed.
"Not her," I said,
nodding my head.

SWIPSY CAKEWALK

When you rang I was washing
my trombone;
in seventh position and slide
right out, it just fits the bath.

Suds in the bell,
then rinse with gel, rub down
and dry, then polish it well.
Time for a tune. What will
it be? Careless Love
– played in C?

What's that you say? Either me
or my trombone? Let's see:
Okay, you go. I'll blow.

So now I'm Nobody's Sweetheart;
I always thought
we had A Fine Romance;
all right, I promise: There'll Be
Some Changes Made.

I see, you want All of Me;
must I really play Bye Bye Blues?
You used to love Swipsy Cakewalk,
and what about One O'Clock Jump?

Okay, I know, I'm just
a Big Butter and Egg Man.
You know what, you're just
a Hard Hearted Hannah!

Why don't you Come On
and Stomp, Stomp, Stomp;
surely Our Love
Is Here to Stay?

Must I Sit Right Down
and Write Myself a Letter?
Am I just a Stranger
on the Shore?

You say you've had too much
of Blues My Naughty
Sweety Gives to Me;
but isn't that
the Glory of Love?

Now I Don't Get Around
Much Anymore.

ODE TO AN OLD ROSE

All dead roses should be dyed;
What do you think Now,
What will you think Then?

Just look: perplexed petals
Drooling off the stem;
Gone is the corolla of concupiscence,
Once pinkly deliquescent
Now darkly dehydrated,
Shuddering at the caress of rain.

But, if you try to represent
This indignity of fading life,
You find in each charred line
And deeply darkened shade,
A noble belligerence
Which shimmers with a sense
Of what has gone before.

So, look down the stem
And see again another rose
Still closed on beauty yet to come.

MAGIC MOMENTS

The dove was always there,
perched above the shuttered
shop where one word
of its former name
could still be seen;
in shimmering paint
it said: M A G I C

And so, with that in mind,
I take you back to the days
when every childhood
dream was dispensed
from that emporium
by a joyful happy couple
whose names we never knew.

How, after being released
from school, we boys
and girls headed for
the store which promised
more than all our hopes
could buy – magic and laughter;
for that is what they called their shop.

And all our pocket
money was well spent
on tricks and jokes
they sold to us –
and pressed into our
grateful hands
when we'd not enough to pay.

We dubbed the wise
and kindly purveyor
of tricks and pranks
our Abracadabra Man,
and saw his pretty
wife as his assistant
in some long-gone
glitzy life of rabbits
and hats and disappearing acts.

If I arrived alone
to browse about their
shop, Mr A would
demonstrate his latest
conjuring trick to me
and his wife applaud
when I'd rehearsed
until perfection;
and, all the while,
the white dove
would be there,
clinging to the rim
of a black top hat.

Then one day I called by
to find the shop all boarded up;
Abracadabra Man
had passed on,
the people said,
and Mrs A had moved away;
but the white dove
lingered there,
messenger of magic,
making our crumbs
all disappear.

SUMMUS SUM!

At school I topped the Latin
class and charged
the other boys and girls
a bar of chocolate
to do their homework
– until the teacher
caught me out and seized
my hoard of fruit and nut.

For punishment he locked
me in his cupboard –
to cure me of my vanity.
"Who makes himself too fine,
breaks himself in fine,"
he said to me. "Now write
that out one hundred times
– in medieval Italian."

READING RIGHT

Looking back with mellowed eye
I see the deeds of shame and gain
which moulded me;
and now, in books,
I find the pride that others
had in lives that built
our history –
and wonder at the smallness
of my own offence.

WOMAN IN THE STREET

I see you pass me by
and how you scowl
when I try
to smile
in your direction

Each time we meet
my heart turns
topsy-turvy
and no pill
can cure
its somersaulting
beat

I tried once
to ignore you
but could still
see you
hard-looking
in my mind

Now I see you
all the time
and dream
that you smile
at my chagrin

as I pick up
courage
to greet you
in the street

I followed once
because
by chance
my business took
me in the same
direction

And then I felt
in knowing
where you went
like a guilty
stalker

So now I never
go
to that part
of town
now curfewed
by imagined
love

SO COOL

In jazz you
hear the colour
see the sound
hunger for
the next blue note

RUNAWAY

I'd practised different voices
to hide the alto ring
and borrowed father's cap
to flaunt that jaunty adult look,
and shaved each day to make
the facial fluff grow stiff
and dark – and sort of sinister.

All ready then, I'd packed a satchel
bag with compass, food and scout
pen-knife (complete with spikey
blade for stones in horses' hooves);
my school atlas and dictionary
of French equipped me for my Odyssey.

After bussing to the Channel ferry,
I planned to hitch a ride the other side
to barracks in Marseille
and sign up as a Legionnaire.

I'd passed a scholarship
for the school my parents
wished for me, but didn't
want to go away from home –

not when I'd lost my heart
to the girl who sat
next to me in class.

I'd read the books of PC Wren
and knew all about the Foreign Legion
and the bravery of their fighting men;
but I only got as far as Dover –
defeated by port police, puzzled
by a passport in my brother's name.

Back home, my parents laughed to hide
their tears and never talked
of how Beau Geste had lost their
man to five years' servitude
in boarding school instead.

END OF THINGS TO COME

Sprinkled from afar
by your confetti thoughts,
I dreamed of happiness;
enjoined, entwined,
we breathed as one,
sated by the clamours
of the night –
for passions are the end
of things to come.

Now, in waking dreams,
I wait for you
– the laughter and the whoopsie-doo –
and times when we are one,
for passions are the end
of things to come.

And when we are together,
we may shout and rant a little
– an amalgam of emotions shared –
but let's not resist
the current of our love,
for passions are the end
of things to come.

That ring I found
with snakes entwined,
I bought with you in mind;
so please, my love,
don't say No;
for passions are the end
of things to come.

But now you've checked
the balance of our
uneven love, you run
from me, without a word,
for passions are the end
of things to come.

So I burn what's left
of us then scrabble
in the flames to rescue
the last picture posed,
blackened legs still
touching on a mountain
side, the climb too
steep for you,
for passions were the end
of things to come.

DEAR BROTHER

We fought a lot –
I the cowboy,
you the Indian who always lost
– and our tough fraternal love
had that vibrant
spontaneity
of the jazz I played
the day you died.

But the tears
just wouldn't stop.

TOGETHER

Being with you
is such ecstasy;
all tenses have become
the one
– passions pulling
silken threads of past,
present and of future
into a triptych
of ourselves.

MY OPERATIC LOVE

After you departed
from my life
with such finality,
the embers of my love
for you took many
months to cool;
and in that time
my dreams at night
sought to re-kindle
glowing hope
with bellows blasts
of operatic impossibility.

One such dream wakened
me into burst of song
as I joined in
the first act finale;

in synopsis, it went like this:

We'd been sailing,
you and I, in our
yacht of love
along the eastern
shores of Africa;

and, if my geographic
recollection be true,
had entered some
great estuary leading
to the darkest heart
of that chaotic continent.

You and I had gone ashore
and you had trod
a different path;
out of sight,
I called your name
but no one came,
so I tracked back
to our sailing boat
to wait for your return,
but found it was nowhere
to be seen; that was
when I woke up singing:
"My ship has gone, my
ship has gone" – with
a chorus in response
informing me: "The pirates
took it, the pirates took it."

The conduct of the second
act took a more convoluted
path as I fell back into sleep
and went in search of you
and found that you'd
become the pirates' moll,

clinging to their king
as if you were his queen.

Naturally I kill him
in a brave fight for
my ship – and the one
I love; and, as I do,
you swoon across his
body with an aria of despair,
shunning me with
your piratic tears.

And so die the embers
of my love for you,
in operatic confusion
and a very minor key.

SEEN BUT NOT HEARD

Rather I would write
my tale on running
water than tell
it you who are
so loath to listen

TALES FROM WALES

HARDY MAN

Into the house
the hardy man came
from the field;
no word was said
as he stomped
his mud boots
on the slate-slatted floor,
while his wife
fussed over his tea.

No word was said
as he tore at the bread
with his split spaded nails,
clay-grouted
from scrauping potatoes
all rain-sodden day.

No word was said,
not even a sound,
as she watched her man eat,
her thoughts not of pity –
or even disgust,
but of pride and of dread
for his new job next week
was under the ground.

No word was said
but she knew that
each day she'd pray
for her mining man's
safe return.

Then, as he supped
at his tea,
their eyes challenged
and held in a love
that would meld
them as one.

"Don't worry, my dove,
I'll always be coming
back home to thee."

ROWAN BERRIES

Tiny clumps of treasure
dangling from a thread,
just waiting to be picked
– but first sift them
through your fingers,
weigh them in the hand;
knead them, count them if you can.

A blind man doesn't
know their colour
but wills them to be bright;
not quite orange,
nor yet red
– vermillion, I'd have said.

UNCLE IDWAL'S SHED

The notice on the shed
door said: Danger Keep Clear
– and I knew it was
addressed to me;
Uncle Idwal was up
to something very queer.

I'd been inside his
brightly-painted wooden
hut, which matched
the yellow gorse below
the hillside garden.

On secret, peeking
visits I'd marvelled
at his world of mad
inventions and hand-built
grown-up toys.

Like his steam-powered engine,
heated into puffing,
piston-pumping jounce
by a burning tray
of purple methylated spirit
from a big brown bottle
marked: Poison. 50 fluid ounce.

Or rows of clicking
fishing reels and split-cane
rods he'd fashioned
for our forays to the river
bank; there we'd cast
the gaudy flies he'd tied
himself to fool the trout.

And, on the bench
for all to see,
two-valve radios
and crystal sets
to tune in to the BBC.

Then, high above and out
of reach, rows
of empty cartridges
he'd stuff with
homemade gunpowder
to gee up Guy Fawkes night.

Usually I watched my
uncle as he tinkered
in his shed, and listened
to his wild Welsh tales
of bats and caves
and wizard Merlin's gold.

"If you want to tell
a story, tell it at
a slant," he'd always said.

Now, intrigued by uncle's
danger sign, I knocked
and listened for his call.
"Stay away," he shouted,
"and wait behind the rock"
     – which brings
       me on to

UNCLE IDWAL'S OTHER SHED

It was there that he went
– to the old outside loo –
with a bulging Rinso
box marked BOOM; next
he backed towards the rock,
trailing cables to my feet.

"Now watch," he said,
touching terminals
to an Ever-Ready pack.
There came a noise
like nothing heard before
– a sort of whoomphing
crump, and then a clang.

The shed at the bottom
of the hill, where each
member of the family
had sometime sat in blissless,
freezing necessity,
stood smoking, wantonly askew,
now bared, hypethral, to the sky.

Down the hill towards
the house, a bucket lay

where it had fallen
from on high,
just by aunty's
flapping sheets,
hand-washed that day,
now streaked and spotted
with what looked like clay.

"Hell's bells," exclaimed
my uncle, as we peered
around the rock,
"what will I say when
she comes home for tea?"

HOMECOMING

Although we never loved,
you gave me strength
when I was lost
and showed me other ways
to live alone once more.

I came to you at Croesor
and found a welcome
only Wales can give
– drawn back by rock
and stream and memory
of glowing mountain light.

Born on Moel-y-Gest,
I longed to see once more
that rugged, sharp profile
of dark Cnicht and climb
the path of Tryfan
or cross Crib Goch in snow
and row the Menai Strait
then feel the wash of rain,
knowing that the sun
would shine on me again.

TRAPPING FAIRIES

From technicolour dreams
I woke to find the cold
slate floor beneath my feet
as I sleeping-walked
about my aunty's home.

The scene my childish
eyes discerned, and painted
on my mind for decades
of immediate recall,
was of my grown-up
cousin fashioning a snare
he said would catch him
rabbits for the pot.

And this gave me an idea
beyond my age when
fairies still held
me in their thrall.

For if a bunny caught
the noose around its
neck, why not one
of the little tykes
my aunty said had

trampled down her
flowers by moonlight?

If only I could catch
me one and ask it why
it was so small
and if it would grow
the size of me and,
if a girl, perhaps then
I could steal a kiss.

And so, next day, I took
my cousin's snare and
baited it with birthday
cake and left it
out at night
in the daisy dingle dell.

In the morning I awoke,
without doing another
walking-sleep, and went
to check my fairy trap.

The cake had gone,
but there was a little
speck of blood upon the grass.
Oh, I was heart-broke,
thinking I had hurt
the little foogaloo
when I only thought
to have a chat.

Now, in adult life,
I wonder if the tiny
folk have put
a curse on me.

COOKING THE BOOKS

The boy hovered
at the kitchen door,
hungry for his tea,
wondering what's in store.

His mother, unaware,
was toiling at the sink;
then, wiping her hands,
she moved towards the stove.

The boy, me – her son,
watched expectantly.
She bent, oven cloth held forth;
but instead of pie or bread,
she drew out two books – both red.

They're from the library, she said.
Your grannie likes to heat them up.
– Why? I said, with a puzzled shake of head.
– To kill the germs that borrowers have left,
that's why, she said.

Next day, at Sunday lunch,
I couldn't eat my meat
– not with other people's
germs hiding in the roast.

Dear gran, she died aged 94;
two oven-ready books
still in her shopping bag
– and the germs live on ...

SILVER ADDER

Coiled fatly on a rock,
the adder sucked in strength
from the body-heating sun
and made ready for the hunt.

Its squat, arrow head
hid folding fangs,
ready primed with searing
yellow sting – enough
to stop a rabbit dead.

The only movement came
from its deeply-forked
black tongue as it
licked the scent of prey
from off the mountain air.

Along its stubby length
a dark zig-zag
announced its
viperous identity.

Meanwhile, a buzzard circled overhead ...

The snake, a silver
mutant, not the usual
bracken-brown, melded

in so well with its
grey bog habitat.

And on the other side of the rock ...

A young boy sat near,
unaware,
as he listened
for the noise that brought
him to the heather
hummock by the rock.

Soon it came, a distant hum
that rent the sky,
increasing in intensity
as vibrations shook
the dry cracked earth.

The adder couldn't hear
the deafening drone,
but felt the thrumming sound;
slowly, it lifted its brutal
head, swaying side to side
as its tongue tasted air.

Coiled tightly now,
it sensed the smell
of prey; but still
its coral-black eyes
could not find the target,
hidden by a tussock hump.

The boy looked up
and saw the aeroplane
– Flying Fortress, four
engines (reciting to himself),
B-17, crew of ten,
nine-bomb capacity.

Behind the bomber came
seven more, but that
was all (four missing,
thought the boy).

His sadness grew
as the planes flew on;
and then he saw
a fluttering sheen of silver
as tiny strips of radar-fooling
screen cascaded down to him.

One fell upon the adder's
rock and the boy
reached out in search of it.

His cry of pain
was drowned
by the sound
of the last returning plane.

And as the striking adder
crawled away,

the circling buzzard
swooped on the spent, fat snake
and soared aloft
with its poisoner prey.

The boy, trying not to cry,
staggered down the hill,
clutching his swelling
hand which still held
the silver from the sky.

CAVE PAINTINGS

In vans and trucks marked
CHOCOLATE, the old masters
came in convoy – Wales
their destination from galleries
of blitz-hit London town.

Churchill's orders said
they must be safely stored
in caverns deep beneath
a mountain, away from Hitler's
undiscerning bombs.

Slate mines of Blaenau
became their hiding place,
Blake's mad King of Babylonia
alongside Van Dyck's Charles I,
on horseback underground.

Now they're all back home
again, hanging in the light
at the National and the Tate,
dusted down and shining
– until the next time round.

GOODBYE

And so I fawn from
your tight-rationed love,
from your abacus
count of kisses;

And so I see you
seeing me
hesitate, back off
like a snake
that declines to strike
for conquest's sake
and crawls into the place
it makes its own;

And so I stand, desolate,
like a Punch without
a Judy, on a rain-lashed
beach at Llandudno.

FIRST MEMORY

He said he was my father,
the man in the khaki coat,
and let me pull
the trigger of his gun;
a Lee Enfield .303, I know
that now, used to kill
the enemy far across the sea,
while I was home with Mum.
I called him Daddy –
and I remember that he cried,
silently,
as snow fell on his head.

JONES THE COAL

Rat-a-tat-tat
came his knock
on the door –
and with it
the gift of a song:
"Trumpeter, what
are you sounding now ... "
And we knew it was
Jones the Coal;
for his baritone
voice always came
with the sack
of shiny jet
lumps of fuel.
Jones our black Santa,
he brought welcoming
heat to the cold
of our hilltop home.

YELLOW

Peering through bog myrtle
beside the rocky river's edge,
I see a flash of yellow –
a wagtail whisking water
for insect sustenance.

Its sunshine colour
warms the mind to spring –
and the jubilance
of celandine and gorse
and nodding daffodil.

TALES FROM IRELAND

CORMORANT BOY

No words he ever heard
or spoke – the beaky,
gangly boy taunted
for his hearing loss.

He spends the days away
from bruising human company,
finding kinship with
the kinder ways of nature.

In silent, solitary walks
he senses all about him
and sees and feels what
noisy people miss.

One day, he happens on a cave
behind a waterfall
and wonders at the shimmering
gauze of mist that shuts him
from the world he left.

Ahead of him he scrapes
his way through tunnels
in the gleaming rock
until a light before
reveals a shelf above the sea.

Now he sits there staring
at the sun, a darkened silhouette
among cormorants who bring fish
and leave them at his feet.

For centuries, they say,
he's kept a vigil
from the cliff;
buachaíll cailleach dhubh
they call the rock.

I'll take you there
if you dare to brave
the waterfall like that
lonely cormorant boy.

And if you listen you can hear
the speaking waves
as they well against the cliff:
Buachaíll cailleach dhubh,
buachaíll cailleach dhubh ...

FAITH TRAIN

The woman made the sign
of a cross as the train
sped past the trees
– and I wondered why;
until the curving
change of scene
revealed a distant
church, invisible
'til then.

She'd passed
that way before
and, doubly
steadfast in her
faith, had known
the place
of prayer
would still be there.

BURIED PLEASURE

Places mean a lot to us,
and never more so than when
entrancement of a moment
can be shared with someone else.

The spraints I leave to mark
the spot for future co-joined
interest are buried wines
of tasteful vintage quality.

Look, beneath the moss and ferns
of Killincooly, in dappled shade
there lies a Médoc, seasoned
Bordeaux, lodged in cleft of rock.

Or join me at Tacumshin
Lake to drink my Muscadet
and watch arctic terns
dip and flake the surface in display.

Carrickbyrne's a charming spot,
so what about a hidden Hock
before you clamber up the hill?

Asti Spumante for airy Inistioge
and for Tintern Abbey a Chablis
– or was it Montrachet? –

Tales from Ireland

I forget, I lost the map
where X marked the burial site.

Crossfarnogue and Ballynaclash,
Owenduff River and Curraghmore
all have Sancerre stashed
down there – a fruitfulness
to suit their moods of peace.

Rioja at sandy Raven Point
and Alsace Riesling in Fethard-on-Sea;
no ordinary plonk for Graignamanagh's
Sillare Rock, my favourite
Fleurie's laid down there.

And here, in wooded Edenvale,
a white Macon perfectly suits
the trickledown, dickledown
streel of the Sow.

So, if you see me prowling
with my trowel and hear
the clink of drink,
you'll know I'm on another
vintage spree; do join me then
before discerning worms
can penetrate the cork.

But one thing sure I know:
you cannot bury bottles
in a panoramic sky, like

the rosé-rumpled duvet
swaddling sleepy Enniscorthy.

Instead, you fix the gaze
and paint the scene
upon your mind for later
telling over wine or beer
in some hostelry of love.

AUTUMN DAYS

From sleep you rise
to sound of distant guns
and will the birds
to fly too high
for scattered lead
to shake them from the sky.

You see the rooks,
black leaves deployed
among the trees –
waiting, waiting
on the wind that fans
the buds of Halcyon.

And feel the gentle touch
of broken cobweb
drifting on the breeze,
towing hitch-hike spiders
with trapeze ease.

Now, on the meniscus
of your mind, you hear
the pat of leaf and cobnut fall
and glimpse, on lady's mantle,
dew drops held in diamond thrall.

You listen to a robin's
sweet, more tuneful,
song of equinox
and watch a charm
of finches – golfsock gold
and red and green –
as they cluster round
the teasel scocks.

And yet still you yearn
for your time to sing –
for the tom-tit twitter
of an early spring,
the tartar taste
of wake-up time.

IN HAWKEYE'S FOOTSTEPS

Astride my cottage roof
fixing slates,
I saw him pass,
pebble glasses glinting
in the sun,
towel tucked
underneath his arm.

Hawkeye was off
to the little
sea trout river Finn.

I knew he would
be heading down
the bealach
to Farley's Hole,
my favourite
casting spot.

And I knew what
he was up to,
because at times
like these he never
wore his wig.

Red it was,
bought years ago
from some travelling
hairpiece salesman
who'd caught other
balding villagers
of vulnerable vanity.

Hawkeye's jaunty wig,
much darned with
claret whipping thread,
was always left
at home on these occasions.

Arriving at the bank,
he'd unravel the towel
and take out a net;
wading in, he'd rope
it to a sally branch
in a tunnel
of overhanging trees.

It would be high
tide now and he'd
be back in the morning
to shake out his catch.

I knew, because once
I'd followed him;
what HE didn't know

was that I would
release the netted
fish before he returned.

Sometimes I'd leave
him a couple,
just to allay
his suspicions.
That was twelve
years ago;
now he's gone.

He went out, suddenly,
the poacher's way,
lamping rabbits
in the field above.

Now it is
I who have the net
– and use it to protect
my currant bushes
from the greed of birds.

ECLIPSE OVER EDENVALE

At the eleventh minute
of the eleventh hour
on the eleventh day,
a muzzy sun peeped
from between the clouds
and was momentarily bruised
by the shadow of the moon.

It cast an eerie twilight
over sleepy Edenvale –
such rare crepuscularity;
all creature-breath
bated by this moony sun.

A lone female kestrel hawk,
motionless on the long-dead
apple tree, made an audience
of two as we waited
for the healing of the light.

The racing moon, reason
for this daunting darkness,
sped through its arc
and life sprang back
like a wind-bent birch.

Cascading brightness
bathed us now,
and once again
the hushed birds
began to stir.

August 11, 1999

LAKE OF THE BEAST (LOCH NA PÉIST)

The puddle I found garnered
in a ridgy rock became
for me, in boyhood
fantasy, my Loch na Péist,
except that she – a Hairy
Molly – lay stranded
on an island, waiting
for the sun to dry
her way to heather home.

Stepping stones, placed close,
failed to wake
that slothful ball,
and when, eventually,
I prodded with a twig,
she rolled right in,
and drowned;
so now the beast
was in the boy,
urging him:
Destroy, destroy.

Maggots which he loved
to pull and break
and mutilate,
and conies snared,

and plump-voiced pigeons
blasted from the trees,
all led, decades on,
to loves betrayed
by restless eye;
pace Emer, Carmel,
Kate, Sínéad ...

Beastly Moll, did you
really have to die?

WATCHERS

Mizzen tail held high, the distant
watcher side-stepped on the branch,
prating all the while, drawing
other magpies to its grandstand view.

Soon there were two – but not for joy
with what they had in mind;
sorrow beckoned to the object
of their gorgon gaze.

For on the broken bridge below,
another bird of black and white
flitted through the morning mist,
bearing shags of moss
to chosen nesting site.

The shapely little dipper,
that curtsied constantly,
would never live to see
the hatching of her eggs.

SAGACIATING

In the shadows of the bar
sat two hunched men
nodding in complicity

Times were better
then than now
nodding in complicity

Self-help yesterday
meant helping other selves
nodding in complicity

Hardship shared
meant hardship halved
nodding in complicity

There they sat, becapped,
knitting proverbs,
sagaciating over
white-bearded beer

ROAD TO NOWHERE

Canvassing is not an easy
thing to do – particularly
when the candidate is you;
or so I found when husting
on the road to nowhere.

People Before Party was my
independent stance,
a slogan true
to individuality
as I tramped the streets
and drove and cycled
round eleven counties
with my 'thirties map
to places changed in name
and roads that took
another route.

Posters staring
down at me in colours
of adversity – red and blue
and green and gold – left
me feeling less than bold.

One in particular,
a presidential-looking
ma'am, gave me jiff
at nights, intruding
as she did into my
dreams and stealing
all the votes.

From Head of Hook to
rusting dignity
of posh Greenore,
I traipsed about and did
the soapbox bit in nearly
every town, bar Wexford,
where I couldn't face
the Bullring beasting
from comrades who'd
no brief for me.

But in Moate, epicentre
of this great nation free,
I found true friends
who believed without
plámásing me.
One man, ironically,
who promised me his
Number One was
sitting in the sun
enthralled by Conrad's
Heart of Darkness.

"The horror, the horror,"
I cried in jest – but he
said he hadn't reached
that bit, so I must
have spoiled it all for him.

When, emboldened, I headed
up the big wide street,
I felt like the Pied
Piper with my knot
of followers in tow.
Thank you, Moate,
even though your promises
did not bear fruit.

In Greenore, my most northern
port of all, I threw
pebbles in the sea,
calling out the names
of each county and willing
them to root for me.

Alas, I wasn't voted in,
but fun it was, I enjoyed
the call and learned
how good all people
are – sharing taxing
times that we now
face; so my road
to nowhere did lead me
somewhere after all.

DIPPERS OF KILMUCKRIDGE

The preacher man came
in his square Austin Ten
and parked by
Kilmuckridge pond.

His words were so right
and his eyes sparkled bright
with certain belief
as he spoke of beyond.

People listened,
and stayed – not so
the poor priest;
he passed them all by,
his sightline set high.

When the preacher man
offered them
five bob a dip,
a queue quickly formed
of God-fearing men.

Into the pond
they each took their turn
in the wake
of Saint John,

then off to the bar
with the preacher
man gone.

PAPER TRAIL

At five o'clock
down Royal Avenue
they come,
the black battalions
– wheeled, umbrellaed
kiosks of the Belfast
Telegraph, now distributed
around the city,
feeding us with news
to gossip on;
but not of bombs
these days, it's just
about the flag that tells
of pride for some
or taunts the rest
with troubled history.
A paper trail
to mark the end
of a working day.

FOR THE RACKARD

In Simon's Bar they picked
on the bow-tie man
and the hard ribbing began.

But I didn't know
that it was all show
and sides were drawn
in josh of me, the blow-in boy
who just couldn't see the joke.

Bow-tie man gave out
too with fierce blue eye
of one who'd hurled
against the dairy
door and helped
his county into history.
Years on, I got to know
that bow-tie man
and he became a friend,
I'm proud to say.

His name was Billy Rackard;
now he's gone from Wexford
but not forgot;
as in the field, his fearless
brothers kept a place for him.